HEROES AND HEROINES

of the
OLD TESTAMENT

Bible stories retold for children

Heroes and Heroines of the Old Testament

© 2023 North Parade Publishing,
Written by Janice Emmerson
Illustrations by QBS Learning

Published by North Parade Publishing, Bath BA1 1LF, United Kingdom

All rights are reserved. No part of this publication may be reproduced, stored in a retrieval system or transmitted in any form or by any means, electronic, mechanical, photocopying, recording or otherwise, without the prior permission of the Publisher

Printed in China

Contents

Moses, God's Special Leader — 4
Exodus 1–20

Joshua and the Promised Land — 8
Joshua 5–6, 10

Two Brave Women — 12
Judges 4

Samson, the Strong — 14
Judges 13, 16

The Shepherd Boy — 18
1 Samuel 16–17

The Wisdom of Solomon — 22
1 Kings 3

Daniel in Exile — 24
Daniel 1–3, 6

Brave Esther — 28
Esther 1–8

Moses, God's Special Leader

The Hebrews were slaves in the country of Egypt. And now Pharaoh, the king of Egypt, had ordered the death of any newborn Hebrew baby boy! Moses' mother wrapped her baby in a blanket and placed him in a basket, which she set amid the swaying reeds that grew on the edge of the Nile River. Maybe a miracle would happen and he would be safe!

Pharaoh's daughter found baby Moses and decided to keep him. When he grew up, God had a very special role for him—Moses was to lead his people out of Egypt to the Promised Land!

God told Moses to go to Egypt, along with his brother Aaron. There he was to tell Pharaoh to let the Hebrews go. Not surprisingly, Pharaoh refused, so God sent ten terrible warnings to persuade him.

First, God told Aaron to strike the River Nile with his staff and instantly the water turned to blood. After that the whole country was covered in frogs! For the third warning God sent a plague of gnats, and next came a plague of flies, then a horrid disease that killed all the animals of the Egyptians. Then the Egyptians found their skin covered with boils—itchy, painful boils. Next, God sent a dreadful hailstorm, which was followed by a swarm of locusts. And then God sent total darkness to cover Egypt for three whole days.

But the tenth plague was the worst of all, for it killed every firstborn son in Egypt, from the son of Pharaoh himself to the son of the poorest servant. But God showed the Hebrews how to keep themselves safe, and none of them died. At last Pharaoh agreed to let them go.

The Hebrews finally left the country that they had been in for hundreds of years! Now they were on the move again—heading to the Promised Land, a wonderful land of milk and honey.

But Pharaoh had had a change of heart. He decided to get the Hebrews back, and set off with his army in swift pursuit.

The Hebrews were terrified for they had reached the shore of the Red Sea, and the way ahead was barred by the water. But God told Moses to raise his staff and stretch it out over the sea. And when Moses did as God commanded, the waters in front of him parted. All night God drove the sea back with a strong wind, and a wall of water rose up on either side, leaving a dry path ahead. Then the Hebrews travelled across the Red Sea, without getting even a tiny bit wet!

Pharaoh's army followed hard on the heels of the Hebrews, and as soon as they were all on the path, God closed the waters together again, and every last one of them was swallowed up by the sea. But the people of Israel reached the far side safe and dry—and free. And there they gave thanks to God for all he had done.

Now Moses led his people across the desert. It was a hard journey, but God was with them. Whatever they needed, he gave them. He made sure that they always had enough food and water.

He also gave them some very special rules to help them to get along with one another in peace. He spoke to Moses on the top of a mountain, and when Moses came down to his people, he brought the commandments with him, engraven on two stone tablets.

Moses lived a long, long life. Though he never stepped foot in the Promised Land, he saw it from the top of Mount Nebo before he passed away.

Joshua and the Promised Land

Joshua stood on the banks of the mighty Jordan River. The river was in flood, and there wasn't a bridge in sight. But God had told him that today he was to lead the Hebrews into the Promised Land!

Joshua told everyone to gather together their things and be ready. Then he told the priests to lift up the Ark of the Covenant, which held the stone tablets, and to go ahead. Straight ahead—into the river!

As soon as the first toe of the first priest touched the raging river the waters parted. To one side was a huge wall of water, but ahead of them was dry ground! The priests crossed half-way, and then all the Hebrews walked across the riverbed to the other side.

When everyone had crossed, Joshua told men to gather twelve stones from the riverbed, and he made a special monument out of them to remind the Hebrews how God had brought them across the River Jordan.

Yet another hurdle stood before Joshua and the land that God had promised his people. The walls of the city of Jericho were thick and strong and tall. And when the people inside had heard that the Hebrews were headed in their direction, they had locked the gates. And thrown away the key!

The Hebrews had no siege engines, or cannons, or even ladders. However, they did have God! God told Joshua exactly what he wanted him to do. For six days all the armed Hebrew men marched once around the city. In front of them went seven priests carrying trumpets, ahead of the Ark of the Covenant.

On the seventh day they marched around the city walls seven times. On the last time round the priests sounded a loud blast on their trumpets, and Joshua told all the Hebrews to shout out loudly. And as the soldiers shouted and the priests trumpeted the walls of the city began to quiver and shake, and then the walls collapsed in a cloud of dust!

Then the soldiers charged in and took the city!

And the story of how God had delivered Jericho to the Hebrews was passed throughout the land, and people were afraid.

Joshua and his soldiers were fighting against the Amorites. They had come to the rescue of the people of Gibeon who were under attack. The Hebrew soldiers were brave, and fought hard, and God sent down huge hailstones from the heavens—Joshua could see that they were well on the way to winning the battle.

But night was approaching fast. The battle would not be over before the sun fell behind the horizon. But Joshua really wanted to get this battle over and done with.

Joshua looked towards the heavens. "Sun," he shouted, "stand still over Gibeon. And you, moon, stand still over the Valley of Aijalon!"

And the sun and the moon both stopped where they were, and the Hebrews won their battle! Just because God listened to Joshua!

Two Brave Women

For years the Israelites had suffered at the hands of King Jabin of Canaan, and the commander of his armies, General Sisera. God took pity on them, and spoke to their leader, a woman named Deborah. Deborah had a soldier named Barak gather an army of ten thousand men. She told him that with God's help she was going to deliver Sisera and all his soldiers right into his hands. Deborah trusted God.

But Barak was worried, for his men were not properly trained, and they didn't have enough weapons. General Sisera's army had better weapons, better training—and many, many more men!

He agreed to lead the army into battle—but only if Deborah went with him! He didn't have faith in God. Deborah told him that because of his lack of trust the honour for the victory would go instead to a woman, and not to him!

The Israelites met Sisera and his chariots on the slopes of Mount Tabor. The Canaanite forces were thrown into confusion when their chariots became stuck in the mud. The Israelites fell upon them, and by the end of the day not a single enemy soldier was left standing on the battlefield.

The Israelites had won, just as Deborah had promised, but in all the confusion General Sisera slipped away unnoticed, and returned, angry and dismayed, to the army camp, where he made his way to the tent of one of his allies. There a woman named Jael let him in, and gave him a drink, and told him where he could lie down and rest.

But Jael didn't like Sisera. In fact, she hated him! As soon as the general fell asleep, she took a tent peg and a hammer and used them to kill him!

When news spread of the death of Sisera, Jael was celebrated and honoured for her bravery and for her role in saving the Israelites from their enemy.

Samson, the Strong

There was once a man named Samson who was strong—really, *really* strong! He was so strong that he once overpowered a wild lion with his bare hands! When he was born, his parents promised God that they would never cut his hair. It showed that he belonged to God.

At that time the Hebrews were tormented by their enemies, the Philistines. Samson did everything that he could to be a thorn in the side of these Philistines. He carried out many raids and attacks, and the Philistines grew well and truly frustrated with him. How could he be so strong? They were desperate to know where his unbelievable strength came from. And when Samson fell in love, they seized their chance.

Delilah, the woman that Samson fell in love with, was very beautiful, but she wasn't very loyal. The Philistines offered her silver if she would find out the secret of Samson's strength. Delilah said "yes".

Samson, however, didn't prove very keen to divulge his secret. He kept on telling her different reasons—but none of them were true! In the end, she became very irritated.

"How can you say you love me when you obviously don't trust me?" she whined. "All you want to do is make me look foolish! If you really loved me you would tell me." And she went on, and on, and on about it until Samson could stand it no longer.

To shut her up, Samson finally told her that he had been dedicated to God before he was born, and that he had never had his hair cut. "If someone were to cut my hair," he said wearily, "I would be as weak as any other man." And he hoped that she would finally leave him alone.

But of course, Delilah had no such intention.

When Samson next awoke it was to find his hair shaved and his strength well and truly gone. The Philistines took him away, tore out his eyes, and placed him in chains. But soon his hair started to grow back …

Some time later the Philistine rulers held a huge celebration in their temple, attended by thousands of people. They told the guards to bring out Samson so they could make fun of their old enemy. Samson was placed between two mighty columns which held up the temple.

While the Philistines laughed and drank and ate, Samson prayed to God to give him strength one final time. Then he took hold of the columns, one to his left and one to his right, and he pushed with all his might. The columns groaned and creaked, and then, with an almighty thunder, the columns fell and the temple collapsed on Samson and everyone else that was there!

In this final act, Samson killed more Philistines than he had done in the rest of his lifetime.

The Shepherd Boy

David was just a simple shepherd boy, but God had chosen him to be the future king of Israel. His father, Jesse, had eight fine sons, and when Samuel the priest arrived at his house, he was certain that the eldest son would make a fine king, for he was handsome and strong.

But God told Samuel, "You are looking at the outside, not the inside. Don't judge by appearances."

One by one, Jesse brought forward his sons. But each time God told Samuel that this was not the one. At last Jesse sent for his youngest son, David, who was out in the fields with the sheep.

God said straight away, "This is the one. Anoint him!"

It would be a while before David would take the throne, but from that day onwards the spirit of the Lord was with David always.

Time passed, and the Israelites were at war with the Philistines. David took food to his brothers in the army. The camp was in turmoil, for their enemy's champion, Goliath, had challenged the Israelites to a duel—and Goliath was practically a giant! He was fierce and strong, and the Israelite soldiers were quaking in their boots.

When David heard about it, he said, "Let me go. I will fight him. He has no right to make fun of the army of God."

The king looked at the boy in disbelief. "How can you possibly fight Goliath? You're just a boy!"

"I might only be a shepherd boy," replied David, "but I am used to protecting my sheep. I'm not scared. God will be with me."

The king agreed to let David accept the challenge. He offered him his own armour and sword, but instead David found five smooth stones, and taking these and his sling he went to face the Philistine.

Goliath laughed when he saw him coming. This shepherd boy was his opponent? The Israelites must have lost their minds!

"Don't think I'll go easy on you," he jeered. "When I've finished with you, I'll feed your body to the birds and wild animals!"

David stood before him bravely. "You have your armour and your spear and your sword. But I have God! You shouldn't have said all those bad things about him. Today God will let me defeat you. And it is *I* who will feed *your* body to the birds and animals. Along with the rest of your army!"

Goliath was furious. How dare this little upstart talk to him like that? He moved forward with his sword ready, but David was faster.

Approaching the warrior at a run, David deftly put one of the smooth stones in his sling, swung it expertly around his head, and fired it straight at Goliath.

David's aim was unerring. It hit the giant right in the middle of his forehead—right between the eyes. Goliath fell to the ground, face first! Then David took Goliath's own sword, and used it to cut off his enemy's head!

When the other Philistines saw the fall of their champion they were filled with fear and fled the battlefield. David had saved the day.

And that is how a young shepherd boy defeated Goliath with just a stone and a sling (and God's help, of course!)

It doesn't matter how small and unimportant we might feel, nor does it matter how those around us see us. God has a role for all of us! He can use each and every one of us to carry out his work!

The Wisdom of Solomon

Solomon was the son of David. Soon after he had been crowned, Solomon was visited by God in a dream. "What would you like me to give you, Solomon?" asked God. "Name it, and it shall be yours."

Solomon did not hesitate. "Please make me wise," he said, "so that I might be a good king like my father, and rule over your people as they deserve. Help me to know the difference between right and wrong."

God was pleased. "You might have asked for riches or power or long life," he replied, "You have asked for wisdom, and you shall have it—but you shall have all the other things you didn't ask for too! Follow in my ways and you will live a long and prosperous life."

Solomon became famed for his wisdom. One day, two women came to him, seeking his judgement. They had given birth to sons at the same time, and one had died. Now they both claimed that the living child was theirs.

There was no way to tell which was the real mother. Solomon told one of his servants to fetch a sword. "Cut the baby in two," he ordered. "Then each woman may have half of it."

One woman said, "That is fair. Neither of us will have him!"

But the other gasped in horror, "No! Don't harm my baby. Give him to her—but don't hurt him! I beg you!"

"This is the real mother," Solomon said, "for she would do anything to keep her baby safe." Everyone saw how wise and clever God had made Solomon.

Daniel in Exile

The people of Jerusalem had turned from God. He had let their city fall into the hands of their enemy, King Nebuchadnezzar of Babylon, and those who were fit and strong had been taken to Babylon.

Daniel was one of the exiles in Babylon. He came from a good family and was clever and strong. And that was why he, and three of his friends, were specially chosen to be trained to serve King Nebuchadnezzar himself. They lived in the palace and were given the same food and wine that the king was given.

But Daniel spoke to a guard and told him he and his friends just wanted to eat vegetables and drink water—as God had commanded.

The guard was worried that they would become weak and ill, but Daniel didn't give up. He told him to try it for ten days, and the guard agreed. After that time, Daniel and his friends were fitter and healthier than the other young men who had been eating the king's rich food! And so they were allowed to continue.

Some time after this, Daniel was able to explain a strange dream that Nebuchadnezzar had, when none of his advisors or sorcerors were able to help (partly because the king refused to tell them his dream!)

God told Daniel that the dream—of a huge statue, with a golden head, chest of silver, hips of bronze, legs of iron, and feet of iron and clay, which crumbled into dust when hit by a massive stone which became a mountain that covered the whole earth—foretold the future.

Daniel told the king, "Your dream foretells what will happen after your reign. The head is like the empire of Babylon. The other parts of the statue are empires yet to come, each replacing the one before. But the stone will be a new kingdom that God will set up. This kingdom will destroy all those that have gone before it, and it will last forever! This stone will become a mountain!"

Nebuchadnezzar was impressed. With Daniel, and with Daniel's God. "Your God truly is the God of gods!" he cried, and he made Daniel his chief advisor.

Unfortunately, Nebuchadnezzar soon forgot his good intentions, and built an enormous statue from gold. He ordered everyone to bow down before it. If not they would be thrown into a blazing furnace!

Daniel's three friends refused to bow down before a golden idol—they worshipped God alone. The king was furious, and had his guards heat the furnace up even more, then tie up the men and throw them in. The furnace was so hot that the guards were scorched to death! So imagine how shocked the king was to see the three men moving freely in the flames, along with another man who looked like the Son of God! He called to them to come out—they weren't even sweating!

"Praise your God!" said Nebuchadnezzar. "You were willing to give up your lives to follow his commands and he came and saved you from the fire. There is no other god like him!"

Some time had passed and Daniel was still an advisor to the king, but now it was Darius the Mede who sat on the throne. Darius had taken quite a shine to Daniel, who was clever and honest and trustworthy, and he decided to make Daniel his second in command.

His other advisors were so jealous that they schemed together and tricked the king. Then they set Daniel up. He was caught breaking the law—by praying to God!—and although Darius did not want to, he was forced to send Daniel to the lions' pit.

When the king came to the pit the next day to see what was left of his favourite advisor, he was amazed to see Daniel safe and sound, sitting peacefully among the lions, for God had looked after him.

The king wrote a new law for the people throughout his kingdom, telling them to fear and respect Daniel's God, for he was the one true God, and could perform miracles! Then he threw the other advisors to the lions—and no one saved them!

Brave Esther

King Xerxes of Persia was angry with his wife—he wanted to show her off at a big party he was having and she refused to be put on parade! So he decided to choose a new queen, and ordered his soldiers to find the prettiest young girls in the land, and bring them back to the palace, so that he could choose between them.

One of these girls was lovely Esther. Actually, her real name was Hadassah. It was a Jewish name because she was an exile from Jerusalem. Her cousin Mordecai had brought her up, and he had warned her not to tell the king that she was Jewish. He wasn't sure how it would go down at court. So Esther it was.

There were many pretty girls brought before the king, but Esther was the prettiest, and the king chose her to be his queen.

The king's prime minister was a proud man named Haman. Haman thought very well of himself. He expected everyone else to think very well of him too. He expected people to bow to him, and generally speaking they did—Haman was not the sort of man you wanted to make an enemy of.

When Esther's cousin Mordecai refused to bow—after all, hadn't God told his people only to bow down to him?—Haman decided to have his revenge—not just on Mordecai, but on all Jews. He went to the king and slyly told him that he had learnt that there was a race of people living in his kingdom who refused to honour the king properly. They kept their own laws and didn't obey the king's laws.

Haman tricked Xerxes into signing a decree saying that throughout the kingdom on the thirteenth day of the twelfth month of that year, all the Jewish people living in the empire should be killed!

When Mordecai found out about the decree he was horrified. He sent word to his cousin to plead to the king for the lives of their people. Esther was scared, for it was forbidden to speak to the king unless he sent for you. Indeed, if anyone came to see him without being sent for then they would be killed—unless he held out his golden scepter! So you can see why Esther wasn't keen on going to see him uninvited!

But Mordecai told her that maybe this was exactly why God had made her queen, so that she might save his people!

In the end, Esther was brave enough to go before the king. Happily, he was pleased to see her, and promised to grant her any desire. She was too scared to speak there, so she invited him and Haman to a banquet in her rooms.

At this feast, Esther was still too scared to tell the king the truth, and instead she asked Haman and Xerxes to another banquet the following day! The king was happy to oblige, and Haman felt really pleased with himself, wining and dining with the king and queen!

This time when the king asked her what it was that she wanted, Esther was brave enough to reply, "Please save me! And please save my people! Someone has plotted against us and we are to be wiped out completely!"

"Who would do such a dreadful thing?" asked Xerxes incredulously.

"Our enemy is Haman!" replied the queen, and she pointed to the prime minister!

Xerxes was furious—so furious that he ordered that Haman should be hung!

The first law could not be changed or cancelled, because it had been stamped with the royal seal. However, Xerxes had Mordecai send out a new decree, and this one stated that all Jews had a right to arm themselves, and could fight back if attacked, and destroy their enemies!

So it was that on the thirteenth day of the twelfth month of that year, when the followers of Haman tried to massacre the Jewish people, the Jews fought back and defeated them throughout the empire!

Every year the Jewish people celebrate the holy festival of Purim, and remember how God saved them, through the bravery of Esther and Mordecai.